MAY   2017

Art from the Mart

Kelly Doudna

Consulting Editor, Diane Craig, M.A./Reading Specialist

Published by ABDO Publishing Company, 4940 Viking Drive, Edina, Minnesota 55435.

Printed in the United States.

Credits
Edited by: Pam Price
Curriculum Coordinator: Nancy Tuminelly
Cover and Interior Design and Production: Mighty Media
Photo Credits: AbleStock, Wewerka Photography

Library of Congress Cataloging-in-Publication Data

Doudna, Kelly, 1963-
    Art from the mart / Kelly Doudna.
        p. cm. -- (First rhymes)
    Includes index.
    ISBN 1-59679-449-6 (hardcover)
    ISBN 1-59679-450-X (paperback)
      1. English language--Rhyme--Juvenile literature. I. Title. II. Series.
PE1517.D6 2005
808.1--dc22
                                                                            2005048044

SandCastle™ books are created by a professional team of educators, reading specialists, and content developers around five essential components that include phonemic awareness, phonics, vocabulary, text comprehension, and fluency. All books are written, reviewed, and leveled for guided reading and early intervention reading, and designed for use in shared, guided, and independent reading and writing activities to support a balanced approach to literacy instruction.

Let Us Know

After reading the book, SandCastle would like you to tell us your stories about reading. What is your favorite page? Was there something hard that you needed help with? Share the ups and downs of learning to read. We want to hear from you! To get posted on the ABDO Publishing Company Web site, send us e-mail at:

sandcastle@abdopub.com

SandCastle Level: Beginning

art

cart

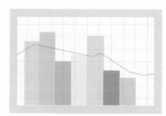

chart

dart

mart

See the  .

Look at the  .

See the 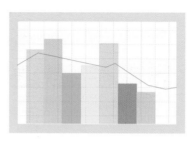 .

Here is a .

Go to the  .

The art is pretty.

The cart is empty.

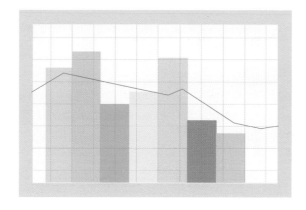

The chart is big.

The dart is blue.

The mart is open.

Art from
the Mart

Bart wants some art.

Bart wants some art from the mart.

Bart uses a chart
to find the art
in the mart.

Bart uses the chart
and throws a dart
to choose the art
from the mart.

Bart puts the chart
and all of the art
he hit with a dart
in a shopping cart
at the mart.

About SandCastle™

A professional team of educators, reading specialists, and content developers created the SandCastle™ series to support young readers as they develop reading skills and strategies and increase their general knowledge. The SandCastle™ series has four levels that correspond to early literacy development in young children. The levels are provided to help teachers and parents select the appropriate books for young readers.

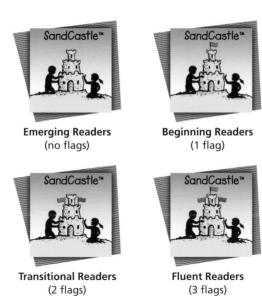

Emerging Readers
(no flags)

Beginning Readers
(1 flag)

Transitional Readers
(2 flags)

Fluent Readers
(3 flags)

These levels are meant only as a guide. All levels are subject to change.

To see a complete list of SandCastle™ books and other nonfiction titles from ABDO Publishing Company, visit www.abdopub.com or contact us at:
4940 Viking Drive, Edina, Minnesota 55435 • 1-800-800-1312 • fax: 1-952-831-1632